Original title:
Living with Unanswered Questions

Copyright © 2025 Creative Arts Management OÜ
All rights reserved.

Author: Charles Whitfield
ISBN HARDBACK: 978-1-80566-142-9
ISBN PAPERBACK: 978-1-80566-437-6

The Veil of Untold Truths

In the fridge, what lurks that smells so spry?
I ask my socks where the other pairs fly.
Is the cat plotting, or is that just me?
Why's the toaster always so full of glee?

Did I leave my keys in a parallel realm?
Or is my brain just stuck at the helm?
Why's the coffee stronger than my desire?
And why do my plants seem to conspire?

Tides of Lingering Queries

Why does the moon look like cheese at night?
Is that why the mice dance in delight?
Do shadows argue when we're not around?
Or is that just fiction my mind has found?

What do squirrels think of during their play?
Do they ponder life or just seize the day?
Is the fridge a portal to the unknown?
And why does my dog steal my favorite bone?

The Puzzle of Untouched Realities

Why do socks vanish, like ninjas unseen?
Is there a sock thief that's clever and keen?
Do fish gossip about our bathing suits?
And do pigeons think they're wearing cool boots?

Is the universe expanding, or just my waist?
Why do I talk to my plants with such haste?
If onions make us cry, what do they know?
And when will my laundry finally grow?

Moments Suspended in Question

Where do lost buttons scamper away?
Are they hiding or starting their own sway?
Why does my hair have a mind of its own?
And why do I daydream of sitting on a throne?

Who decided that cats are the true rulers?
In a world full of dogs, they're the best droolers.
Do clouds gossip while floating so high?
And does the wind laugh as it whispers by?

In Quiet Reflections

Why is the sky blue? I ask with a grin,
As if someone heard me, and where do I begin?
Do fish really know how to swim with such flair?
Or do they just float, showing off their cool hair?

What happened to socks in the dryer's dark lair?
Do they dance with the lint in a magical air?
I ponder and chuckle, in my own little way,
These questions will keep me confused all day!

The Phantoms of What-If

What if the chicken crossed, just to get to the other side?
Or the cow jumped over the moon, in a fun, wild ride?
Do frogs ever wonder if they're really all that wise?
Or are they just hoping for a princess in disguise?

Each 'what-if' floats by, like jellybeans in the breeze,
Are unicorns hiding, or just playing hard to please?
I laugh at these thoughts, such a silly parade,
In a world full of mystery, it's a fun charade!

Cracks in Certainty

If two is company, why is three a crowd?
Do clouds ever complain when they're wrapped in a shroud?
Can a tree really sneeze if it catches a cold?
Or is that just a tale that never gets old?

The certainty cracks, like eggs in a pan,
I wonder if goldfish dream like I plan?
With giggles and questions that float in a stream,
I trip over laughter while chasing the dream!

Resilience in Ambiguity

Why do we park in a drive, but drive on a park?
Is there a secret code hidden in the dark?
Do owls really hoot, or just sing out of glee?
Asking the tough ones like, "Where's the sock for me?"

In the mix of questions, I'm dancing with flair,
Like spaghetti that wiggles and twirls in the air.
Though answers may shimmer like stars in the night,
I'll laugh through the puzzles, it feels just right!

Whispers in the Void

Why does my cat stare at the wall?
Is there a ghost, or is it just small?
I ask him questions; he purrs with glee,
And I ponder if he knows more than me.

The fridge hums secrets in mid of the night,
It laughs as I find my snack isn't right.
Where did the chocolate suddenly flee?
I guess it's a mystery, shared 'twixt you and me.

In Search of the Elusive Truth

I googled my dreams, but found weird maps,
One led to llamas, another to naps.
The more I search for that great, wise sage,
The more I find just a cluttered page.

Why do socks vanish, like they've got a plan?
Do they form a society, where they all can?
I ponder and scratch my bewildered head,
Are they plotting revenge on the shoes that they've led?

Shadows of Curiosity

I found a tadpole and named him Ted,
He hopped on the table; I squealed in dread.
Does he dream of being a frog on a log?
Or is he just plotting to eat my new dog?

My coffee goes cold while pondering fate,
Did I leave it there, or is time just late?
Each sip is a riddle, a quest and a jest,
And I laugh at the chaos, for that's the best!

The Space Between Answers

The toaster pops up a slice, all burnt,
"Is this breakfast or the culinary world's worst?"
I look in its slots, searching for clues,
But all that I see are old crumbs and blues.

In the garden, my plants talk in whispers so loud,
Their gossip leaves me both puzzled and proud.
"What do you want?" I ask, and they sway,
But the only answer is the wind's soft ballet.

Beneath the Surface of What-Ifs

What if cats could talk, oh dear?
Would they complain about the beer?
Or simply stare with their wide eyes,
And ask why we're wearing ties?

What if socks unite at night?
To form a band and start a fight?
They'd challenge shoes to dance all day,
While we just laugh and walk away.

What if trees could dance and sing?
Would they teach us the latest swing?
Or would they just sway in the breeze,
And think we're odd for not joining ease?

What if my toast could take a leap?
Would it glide or fall in a heap?
Its mission missed, it's burnt instead,
Yet still, I eat, with crumbs to spread.

Mystery Between the Lines

Why are pencils always in a mess?
They hide from erasers, I must confess.
Each time I write, it's a great chase,
My desk looks like a scribbled place.

How does the clock always lose my time?
It ticks away in a silent rhyme.
I chase its hands, they twist and blend,
I swear we're playing, but where's the end?

Why do hamburgers hide their cheese?
In a blanket of lettuce, with such ease.
They smile so big with their bun-filled grin,
As I wonder what chaos lies within.

Do fish get thirsty, or is that odd?
Do they sip water from their own pod?
In bowls, they swim with fishy cheer,
While I just munch on my grilled deer.

Holding Breath in Uncertainty

Why do shoes get odd in pairs?
One's got flair, the other just stares.
They hang out lonely on the floor,
Plotting rebellion, wanting more.

How can ice cream melt so fast?
Just when I think it's meant to last.
It giggles softly, slips away,
Leaving me craving another day.

Why do sandwiches always fight?
With lettuce tangling, it's quite a sight.
Tomato leaps, but mustard's sly,
As I dig in, they wave goodbye.

How do phones know when I'm near?
They vibrate boldly, give a cheer.
Yet when I call, they play a game,
Ignoring me, it's always the same.

The Uncharted Paths of Why

Why do cats think they're the king?
They prance around, with tails a-swing.
Do they ponder deeply, feel the weight?
Or just knock over my favorite plate?

How does bread become a toast?
Did it dream of crunching from the coast?
It leaps from the toaster, brown and hot,
And I can't help but laugh a lot.

Why do socks fall off the line?
Do they tango, spin, and reel in time?
The laundry lives a life of fun,
While I just wish to find the one.

What's with the cereal's early crunch?
Do they party before I munch?
And when I pour, they make a splash,
A morning dance before the crash.

The Edge of Understanding

Why does the toast always land down?
Surely it's plotting, wearing a frown.
Is it the gravity or just my luck?
Each breakfast feels like a cosmic stuck.

Do fish even know they're swimming around?
Or do they just think it's dry ground?
I ponder these thoughts with a giggle and grin,
As I fill my mind with the chaos within.

What's the sound of one hand that claps?
Or do we need both for those loud slaps?
My thoughts leap like frogs, they hop and they play,
As I muse on the puzzles of my crazy day.

Why's cheese always in a 'grate' mood?
Is it lonely being the milk's brood?
Unanswered conundrums make me chuckle and sigh,
But they dance in my head like a pie in the sky.

Echoes of Longing

Do cats really think they own the whole house?
Or are they just waiting for a quiet mouse?
I'll ask them someday, or maybe just wink,
For my fears about felines are often on the brink.

Why do socks vanish in the laundry's whirl?
Is there a sock party? Do they twirl and swirl?
As I hunt for the mate, I chuckle aloud,
Unanswered threads in my house feel like a crowd.

What does a goldfish dream of at night?
A big bowl of ocean, that feels just right?
With each little splash, I can't help but laugh,
At the tiny fish thinking, "I wish for a giraffe."

Why do we say 'sleep like a baby' so true?
They scream at midnight without a cue!
But in the silence, I ponder this jest,
And wonder if adults won the snore contest.

The Unfinished Symphony

Why's the piano always slightly off-key?
Is it just my ears or its stubborn decree?
As I play with abandon, notes leap and evade,
A symphony tangled like toast in a braid.

What if my dog thinks I'm the oddest fan?
"Look at that human, what's her plan?"
With each wobble and bark, we share a duet,
An unfinished tune full of giggles and fret.

What's the true color of a chameleon's skin?
Do they ever get bored in their colorful spin?
As they change with the breeze, they hide and then blink,
I chuckle at nature as it winks and it drinks.

What makes a cat think it can drive my car?
Is it the power of fuzzy, or just too bizarre?
As I watch it pretend, my heart fills with glee,
In this unfinished symphony of whimsy and free.

The Paradox of Knowing

Why is pizza a circle in a square box?
Is it a food enigma, a chef's paradox?
With each cheesy slice, I ponder the state,
As I devour my worries on a thin crust plate.

How does one fly with a suitcase in tow?
Do wings come from dreams, or just wanting to go?
As I pack my wild hopes into a bag,
I laugh at the thought, it feels like a rag.

What's in a name? Why do words make us laugh?
Is it the silliness, or just the wrong half?
With each quirky phrase that dances on lips,
I dive into laughter and do verbal flips.

Why does my plant seem to judge me each day?
Is it the way that I talk or the way I sway?
In this garden of questions, I plant seeds of cheer,
As I water the nonsense and let go of fear.

Between the Lines of Uncertainty

I asked the clock why time felt slow,
It shrugged with hands that wouldn't show.
The cat is plotting more than I think,
But what he's saying is hard to ink.

A squirrel stares, then runs away,
Is it my look or the games they play?
Life's riddles dance in a funny way,
Like socks that vanish when I do my laundry today.

Threads of Incomplete Stories

My coffee's gone cold, left on the shelf,
Did it dare to leech its warmth by itself?
Ghosts of questions spin in my head,
Could it be that the toaster's misled?

The goldfish glances with bubbles and flair,
Does it ponder the meaning of water and air?
As I scribble my thoughts on a napkin so neat,
The waiter just smirks, then brings more to eat.

Echoes of What Could Be

A shoe on the ground, what happened to its mate?
Is it off on adventures, or just up for debate?
The fridge hums secrets at midnight's call,
While I stand amazed, fumbling through it all.

My phone's buzzing with no one in sight,
Is it searching for answers or just a good fight?
I scribble and giggle at my thoughts so profound,
As shadows of questions wander around.

The Space Within the Question

In a world where socks always go astray,
I ponder their journey, come what may.
Did they meet a cheese fish in the dryer?
Or did they link up with a sock-wearing buyer?

I taste fortune cookies with empty replies,
Do they laugh at my fate, or just tell clever lies?
Philosophers from afar roll their eyes,
While I chase these odd thoughts like a bird in the skies.

A Collection of Maybe

In the fridge, a lunch I made,
Is it still edible? I'm afraid.
That sandwich mocks my indecision,
Was it turkey? Or a strange vision?

I ponder socks that disappeared,
Where do they go? It's quite unclear.
Perhaps they're on a secret spree,
A wild sock life, just fancy-free.

My plant seems fine, or is it dead?
It sways like it's heard something said.
Should I water it? Or give it shade?
The silent drama of leaf parade.

Was that a phone or just a beep?
No message here, just thoughts to keep.
The question lingers, plays my mind,
Oh, what mysteries are left behind!

The Stillness of Unstated Yearnings

Why do I have five spoons at hand?
Am I a chef? Or just unplanned?
Each utensil a question, it seems,
A silver set from mismatched dreams.

I stare at shoes, which pair to wear?
With stripes or polka dots? A flair?
Each choice a riddle wrapped in lace,
Will I trip or just win the race?

The clock ticks loud, what time is it now?
I've lost track—oh, here comes a cow.
Its moo is deep like thoughts in me,
Riddles murmuring on a tea spree.

Did I lock the door? It haunts my steps,
Maybe I did, or maybe I prepped.
The mind fumbles like an old DJ,
Spinning tunes of yesterday's play.

Journeying Through Question Marks

Maps and signs, but where's my road?
The paths, like my jokes, are often bowed.
Did I take a left or just a right?
Each direction feels like flight.

In cafes, my order's gone astray,
Did I mean coffee or 'surprise' spray?
The barista smiles, but I just stare,
Is the latte my first love affair?

I'm tracking snacks through all this doubt,
Is there a cookie in here? Shout out!
Each bite a puzzle, sweet and bold,
Questions whirl like candy sold.

And yet, beneath this silly fuss,
Life's quirky stuff, all made to chuckle us.
With unanswered thoughts, I test my fate,
Embrace the absurd—it feels just great!

Images of Unfamiliar Paths

A road that twists, a path unknown,
Is it a shortcut or overgrown?
I peek around and scratch my head,
What's next? A cat, or perhaps a shed?

My GPS just flipped me off,
Said 'recalculating'—how to scoff.
Do I take a chance on the breeze?
Or stick to places that aim to please?

The bushes rustle, is it a joke?
Maybe a squirrel, or just a bloke.
The world's a stage of puppets grand,
With each new scene, a mystery planned.

Through every turn, I laugh and muse,
Navigating life with quirky clues.
For answers fade like whispers, too,
And I delight in the bemusement view.

Serendipity of the Unknown

Why is my cat staring at the wall?
Maybe she saw a ghost, or a ball!
Life's quirks make us scratch our heads,
Searching for answers in laundry threads.

Do socks really vanish into thin air?
Are they on a vacation somewhere?
I once asked a plant, it looked quite confused,
Not even one clue, I guess I'm just bruised.

Is cereal soup? A thought for the brave,
With spoons in hand, we dig and we crave.
The fridge hums secrets no one can share,
Lost in a maze, is there truth hiding there?

In the garden, weeds dance the cha-cha,
Who taught them rhythms? Oh, who would've thought-a?
We laugh at our questions, all tangled and messed,
In this circus of life, we're all here, just blessed.

The Light in Uncertainty

Why do we trip on sidewalks at night?
The moon's at fault for the wobbly flight!
Wobbly shoes lead to wobbly thoughts,
   Where did I leave my beloved pots?

Did my coffee just wink at me, right?
Or does caffeine just spark this delight?
Every sip brings another wild tale,
Like sails in the wind, we flounder and flail.

Why does spelling 'weird' feel so wrong?
And why sing in the shower with bad songs?
Each note seems to echo through time and space,
   What is that rhythm, oh, what a disgrace!

With puzzles and riddles, the day rolls on,
We might be confused but look at that dawn!
Here's to all quirks in our colorful lives,
In questions, we laugh, and delight surely thrives.

Specters of the Unknown

Ghosts in the closet, or just my old shoes?
I swear they're plotting; what else could they do?
Do they conspire with dust bunnies at night?
Is this a scene from a peculiar fright?

What's with the fridge that groans like my dad?
Is it dreaming of ice cream, or feeling sad?
Each hum is a story, each clink, a new plot,
While I chase my thoughts in a whirlpool of thought.

Do plants eavesdrop on the gossip we share?
Are they just polite, pretending not to care?
They hear all my secrets, my hopes, and my fears,
And yet they stay green through the laughter and tears.

Why do we say 'once in a blue moon'?
Is it a dance or just an odd tune?
We weave in and out of the whims of our mind,
In this ghostly chitchat, some truths we must find.

Lullabies of Loosely Woven Thought

I wonder if clouds have a favorite shape,
Or if they just smile and feel free to scrape.
Do they laugh at our worries from high in the sky?
While we down here ponder, 'Oh why, oh why?'

What would a tomato tell me if it spoke?
Would it complain about being called a joke?
Amidst kitchens and dinners, there's wisdom to find,
As pasta asks bread, 'Are we forever entwined?'

Is it just me or do clocks just conspire?
Ticking in laughter, setting minds on fire.
Suddenly I'm late for a place I won't go,
In this waltz with lost time, we dance to and fro.

So, here's to the twists and the zany and odd,
Questions are puzzles, and life's but a nod.
We chuckle and ponder beneath starlit skies,
In the wackiness of doubts, our joy surely lies.

Footprints in the Fog

I stepped outside, in a misty haze,
Trying to find where my phone stays.
Did I leave it on the couch or the floor?
Or maybe it's hiding, who knows anymore?

My shoes are damp, and so are my thoughts,
Questions swirl round like tangled knots.
Is it Monday, or are we in May?
I guess I'll just guess and hope it's okay.

In fog so thick, I can barely see,
Did I just trip over a ghost or a tree?
Maybe the answers are just out of frame,
But hey, what's the fun in playing that game?

So I dance through the mist, with spirit so bright,
Each wrong turn becomes a delight.
With every lost step, I chuckle and dance,
Unanswered questions? I'll take a chance!

The Lullaby of Uncertainty

Naptime for thoughts, like a hamster on wheels,
Going in circles, yet nothing reveals.
Should I set an alarm or just let it be?
Oh wait, I forgot, do I even need Zs?

Socks on my hands, I'm prepared for the chill,
Do I match them? Or should I just let the thrill?
Should I follow my dreams or eat that whole pie?
Life's little questions make me laugh till I cry.

Like a lullaby sung by a cat on a fence,
I ponder the state of my current suspense.
Is my tea too hot? Or is it just right?
I'll stay up and wonder long into the night.

With a blanket so cozy, I curl up tight,
Chasing the shadows, embracing the light.
Maybe tomorrow I'll figure it out,
But for now, I'll just giggle and shout!

Dancing with Doubt

I put on my shoes in the dead of the night,
Not sure if this is how the dance goes right.
With two left feet, I stumble and sway,
But hey, who needs rhythm anyway?

The clock's ticking loud, or is it just me?
Am I late for a party, or lost in a tree?
Should I bring cake, or is that too much fuss?
The only thing certain is I'm in a rush!

I twirl past my worries, they trip me a lot,
Yet laughter erupts, tying dreams in a knot.
Do I skip the beat, or bounce with the crowd?
In this silent disco, my doubts feel so loud.

In the grand masquerade, I blend with the forms,
Each question unfurling like strange little storms.
So let's raise a glass to the chaos in sight,
While dancing with doubt till the morning light!

Reflections in a Shattered Mirror

I peered in the glass, cracked and so clear,
Wondering why I have broccoli near.
Is it fashion or dinner? I just can't tell,
In this riddle of life, I'll just do it well.

With pieces of glass showing snippets of me,
Would I look better if I were a tree?
Should I park my doubts or let them go roam?
Oh look, here's my sock: it has dreams of its own!

Each shard holds a tale, a quirky delight,
Of moments and choices, both wrong and outright.
As I laugh at my answers, I smile at the mess,
Embracing reflections, I'm trying my best.

In the jigsaw of life, with its chaos of hue,
I'll dance with the fractures and see what they do.
So here's to the questions, the giggles, the cheer,
In this beautiful puzzle, I have no fear!

Veils of Uncertainty

Why do socks disappear as if on cue?
Do they conspire in a socky coup?
The fridge hums secrets, a cold, hushed affair,
Where did that last pickle go? I swear it was there!

Cats sit on windows; they plot and they scheme,
Gazing at nothing, chasing a dream.
Do they know the meaning of life, or just nap?
One blink and I'm lost in their woolly mishap.

What's the right angle to slice a pizza?
Are we destined to eat only the crusts?
Balloons float by with smiles and cheer,
But do they fear the sharp end lurking near?

Where is the remote? Such a classic feat,
Is it hiding 'neath cushions, a soft, cozy seat?
Perhaps it has jumped into a parallel space,
Finding remote-heaven in a cosmic race!

Missing Pieces of Solitude

In my drawer lies an odd sock, too shy,
Is it waiting for love, or just a goodbye?
Mismatched pairs seem to have their own life,
Spinning tales of romance, ignoring all strife.

Teapots whistle like they know the game,
Do they gossip about us? Oh, what a shame!
I sit with my thoughts, a kettle on high,
Wondering if fish feel a need to fly.

Why does my garden grow weeds and not gold?
Does the soil conspire to keep mischief bold?
Bugs throw wild parties, it's all quite absurd,
What's the point of a lawn when it's all just a blur?

Mirrors reflect my bewildered face,
Does it giggle behind me, just out of place?
I ponder life's mysteries while brushing my hair,
Catching a glimpse of a question laid bare!

The Language of Questions

Why do we park on driveways, I ask with a grin?
And why do we never begin at the end?
The fridge whispers tales, it's got secrets galore,
As I search for snacks, always wanting more!

In the yard, the grass giggles under my feet,
Do they share gossip about the sun and the heat?
Turtles move slowly, philosophers in shells,
Are they plotting world changes, or just sharing their spells?

Do clouds ever worry when they float in the sky?
Do they wonder about rain, or just float by and sigh?
The clock ticks away, time on its spree,
But do seconds enjoy such nonchalance, you see?

I ask my cat why she stares at the wall,
Is she seeking the meaning of it all?
As she stretches and naps, my heart swells with glee,
Perhaps the real wisdom is just being free.

A Voyage into Ambivalence

Why do my plants thrive when I give them no care?
Do they like to play hard-to-get with despair?
A garden of chaos, I ponder the mess,
Is that a bloom or a weed? I can only guess!

Rubber ducks float with a pep in their step,
Do they dream of adventures while taking a rep?
Bath time's a party, a splashy delight,
But do they worry what happens at night?

What's the purpose of toast when it falls to the floor?
Is it seeking adventures far beyond my door?
I laugh with my breakfast, it's all in good fun,
And wonder if pancakes just wish for the sun.

Why do the stars twinkle and giggle at night?
Are they sharing jokes, or just feeling light?
In this quest for answers, I join in the play,
Maybe questions are just goofy games we can say!

A Dance with the Unknown

When socks go missing, I start to sway,
Are they off to a party, or lost in the fray?
With every step, I gather a clue,
The secrets of laundry are known by a few.

The fridge hums softly with unspoken doubts,
Is that leftover pizza a treasure or sprouts?
I open the door, the smell makes me grin,
But what's lurking in there? I'm not sure I can win.

The ceiling fan whirls, teasing my hair,
"Who hung those pictures? Who put them up there?"
I twirl and I spin, embracing the jest,
Because life's funnier when we're not at our best.

In corners of chaos, I jiggle and jive,
With each silly question, I feel more alive.
The unknown's a partner who leads me astray,
But oh, how I love this absurdity play!

Fragments of Uncertainty

A half-eaten cupcake is lost in a maze,
Leftover forks start to dance in a blaze.
Who knew that the kitchen could hold such a show?
With every odd moment, I just go with the flow.

The dog looks at me as if I've lost track,
"Where's the ball, human? Now, that's quite a knack!"
I throw it to nowhere, it lands out of sight,
His big puppy eyes say, "Hey, this isn't right!"

My plants whisper secrets that I can't quite hear,
Do they want just water or maybe some cheer?
I'm stuck between sunlight and questionable care,
What's in a fiddle leaf? I'm pulling my hair!

I ponder the meaning of socks with no mates,
Is it fate or a joke that the dryer creates?
Each puzzling moment is wrapped in delight,
I waltz with my questions and enjoy the slight bite.

The Enigma of Tomorrow

A calendar hangs, dates drifting away,
Will Tuesday be sunny or start a buffet?
I flip through the pages with curious glee,
What's planned for this week? It's a mystery!

The weather man chuckles, his forecasts go wild,
Tomorrow could rain or make my hair styled.
I pack for my walks in a raincoat and flip,
But who needs an umbrella when spontaneity's hip?

My lunchbox is packed with items galore,
"Is that jello or pudding? I can't keep score!"
I open it slowly, a game of surprise,
Life's playful moments are just tiny pies.

With worry at bay, I dance to a tune,
Amidst all the questions, I'll chuckle by noon.
Tomorrow's a riddle wrapped in a joke,
At least I'll be ready with a smile and a poke.

Questions on the Wind

The breeze whispers softly, with queries that tease,
"Why did the bird cross the road with such ease?"
With twigs for a crown, he struts like a pro,
Is he auditioning? Wow! That bird really can show!

Clouds drift above like thoughts in my head,
Are they planning a storm or a picnic instead?
I squint at the sky, pondering their game,
Maybe they're fickle, or just feel no shame?

On trips to the store, I wonder and muse,
"Did I need that last item, or am I just confused?"
With every selected snack that I seek,
I leave with a basket and questions that speak.

Each gust that blows carries laughter so bright,
It tickles my mind, fills my heart with delight.
The world spins around, so odd yet so grand,
I'll dance with these questions, hand in hand.

Holding Space for the Unclear

What's that noise? Is it a cat?
A ghost? A squirrel? Or just my hat?
I ponder life in a silly way,
As I chase these thoughts that choose to stray.

Do ducks know why they quack like that?
And why do I wear mismatched socks? A fact!
Each question flops like a fish on land,
While I laugh, wondering where I stand.

I asked my phone, it just replied,
With ads for shoes that don't coincide.
In the realm of what's not so bright,
I find joy in the nonsense of my plight.

In riddles wrapped in giggles and sighs,
I collect uncertainties like butterflies.
Swirling around in the carnival night,
My queries dance, all in delight.

The Horizon of Unsought Answers

Why do I always lose my keys?
They vanish like socks in the breeze.
I wander through thoughts like a lost kite,
Searching for wisdom in broad daylight.

The fridge hums with secrets untold,
Is the lettuce thinking? Or growing old?
I poke and prod like a curious child,
Chasing mysteries, both tame and wild.

A leaky faucet drips a rhythmic tune,
And I think of questions that make me swoon.
Where do old pens go when they disappear?
I'm left with ink that just won't adhere.

The sky is full of clouds, they tease,
Wandering alone, like a squirrel on cheese.
With a chuckle, I muse on the absurd,
Find joy in the quirkiness of the unheard.

When Certainty Takes Flight

I set out on a quest for the truth,
But all I found was a pair of blue shoes.
Were they my size? I'll never guess,
Because now they're my new source of stress.

In conversation with a potted plant,
I pondered hard, but it wouldn't chant.
Do cacti go out on weekend trips?
Or do they stay home with their thorny quips?

A butterfly flits, lost in a thought,
Is it pondering all the matters I've fought?
With wings like questions that soar and twist,
Answers evade like a magician's mist.

Still, I chuckle as I dance with doubt,
It's just a hoodie, not something to shout.
In this circus of queries, I find my art,
As the clowns of uncertainty tickle my heart.

The Garden of Abandoned Queries

In my garden grow thoughts unkempt,
Weeds of confusion where I once leapt.
Each flower's a question, bright and bold,
But the answers are shy, and never hold.

I tend to my doubts like they're sweet peas,
Watering whims with a sprinkle of glee.
Why do plants never tell their tales?
Maybe they're plotting to travel in sails?

And what of the bugs that buzz past my ear?
Are they critiquing my last career?
I shake my head, fall into a fit,
Chasing real answers like a stray bit of wit.

With laughter, I nurture my curious plight,
As the sun dips low, painting it bright.
Each inquiry blossoms, no need for a plan,
In this garden of giggles, I'm the happiest man.

Sifting Through the Sand

Why's the sky blue? I must know,
Like socks that vanish in the wash.
How do cats always steal the show?
I ask the tide, it just says 'posh.'

In each grain hides a secret truth,
Like why my coffee's gone so cold.
Is laughter really just aloof?
Or is it all a spell that's rolled?

Oh, to understand the world so bright,
Like why my pants never seem to fit.
But maybe joy is in the plight,
And questions are just a cosmic wit.

The Hush of Unsung Mysteries

Why do we never say 'see you later'?
Is it just easier to wave?
And what makes chocolate such a traitor?
A monster that we all gotta save?

Why does my cat stare at the wall?
Is there a raccoon plotting up there?
Do the shadows notice my small fall?
Or laugh at my hair's latest dare?

Every tick of the clock brings a grin,
Like whether socks can find their match.
In the game of life, we all win,
Even if answers are hard to catch.

The Haunting of What-Could-Be

Why do ghosts only seek the shy?
Is it the lack of screams they crave?
Or maybe they just want to fly,
  On a lonely late-night wave?

What if my dog could truly speak?
Would he scold me for missing walks?
Or ask for treats, a bit antique,
And share the gossip of other dogs?

Each question's like a playful tease,
That dances on the tip of thought,
But maybe laughter is the breeze,
That turns our worries into naught.

The Horizon of Questions

Why do we ponder on cloudy days?
As if rain can wash us away.
Do ducks ever count how many ways,
To quack at the world, come what may?

Why is a riddle wrapped in rhyme,
Like my socks lost in the dryer?
Is time an illusion in its prime,
Or just a news anchor for the flyer?

With each sunrise, new wonders bloom,
Like where do all the good pens go?
Maybe questions clear the gloom,
Chasing answers with a playful glow.

Tethered to the Undiscovered

I once asked a cloud, where do you go?
It chuckled and drifted, a whimsical show.
A squirrel with a frown, he eyed me quite strange,
As if pondering life's meaning was more than a change.

I chased after shadows, they laughed and they danced,
My socks were all soggy, but hey, I just pranced.
The owls in the trees hooted loud with delight,
As I sought out the answers that slinked out of sight.

A goldfish once winked, as it thought deeply, too,
Its bowl full of questions, with hardly a clue.
I sighed on the ground, feeling quite like a fool,
In a world full of answers, I forgot my own rule.

Then I tripped on a rock, and it whispered to me,
"Some things just don't matter, just laugh, can't you see?"
So I twirled with the daisies, threw caution away,
For in the wild, unanswered, I found joy in the play.

Navigating the Unseen Path

I took a wrong turn on life's winding road,
Bumped into a cactus, it said, 'What a load!'
The map that I drew turned to spaghetti and goo,
Yet the giggles of adventure just pulled me right through.

A raccoon nearby offered me snacks by the tree,
He asked if I knew where I wanted to be.
I shrugged with a grin, took a bite from his stash,
Sometimes questions just hang, but the fun's in the crash.

I sent my GPS straight into the creek,
Mumbled at it softly, 'You're such a bad geek!'
A frog then hopped by, with a crown and a bow,
Said, 'Kings have no answers, just riddle and flow.'

With starlit confusion, we danced on the grass,
Each step a new mystery, we let the night pass.
Unseen paths can be silly, but oh, what a ride!
With laughter our compass, we took it in stride!

Echoes of Unspoken Thoughts

In the cupboard of dreams, I found socks that could sing,
They whispered sweet secrets of absurd little things.
A jellybean army retorted with glee,
As I pondered the greats: what's life's recipe?

A cat wore a crown, declared, 'All hail the night!'
I asked him his wisdom, he scratched, said, 'Not right!'
His purr was a riddle, his tail swayed in tune,
'There's magic in nonsense, just dance to the moon!'

A banana once told me, 'Peel back your strife,
Life's a shadow puppet, a comedic slice of life.'
So I chuckled and twirled, in my polka dot hat,
Even unspoken thoughts wear a funny old spat.

The echoes of laughter bounced high on the walls,
As questions, like balloons, danced, tripped, and had falls.
With humor our sherpa, we trekked on with flair,
In a world full of wonders, we never would care.

The Silence of Questions

A turtle once mused, 'I'm slow, but I shine,'
As I pondered my riddles in exquisite design.
He blinked with a grin, then mumbled, 'What next?'
I shrugged and replied, 'I'm somewhat perplexed.'

An ant held a meeting, declared, 'We adapt!'
Though none knew the topic, they all just then clapped.
I giggled aloud, what a sight it must be,
In the silence of questions, a bustling spree!

A fridge in the corner sang songs of the past,
While sandwich debates waged - hard cheese versus fast.
I joined in the fray with a donut in tow,
For in silence of questions, it's laughter that grows.

The lightbulb above blinked, said, 'Let's make a scene,'
It flickered like 'yes,' as I danced in between.
With whimsical wonders, we played through the haze,
In a world full of questions, let's laugh all our days!

Starlight of Inquiry

Why do socks vanish in the wash?
It's a mystery quite absurd.
Do they dance off on a new journey?
Or just fall for the lint of the world?

Is cereal soup? Who can tell?
A breakfast wonder, we must ask.
Do cows ever stare at the stars?
Or is that too much to unmask?

If a tree falls with no sound,
Does it make gossip without a crowd?
Or do the squirrels shrug in silence,
Laughing at things we've unbowed?

Why do we never eat the moon?
It looks so tasty from afar.
Must we save it for some picnic?
Or is it just a shining star?

The Fabric of Ambiguity

In the fridge, what's that odd smell?
Did the garlic cheat on the cheese?
Is that lettuce plotting a coup?
Or just sad that it wilted with ease?

Why do we press the elevator?
So impatient, we tap and we poke.
But it takes longer than our wishing,
Yet we giggle and share a joke.

How do cats know our secrets?
They sit and stare with their sly eyes.
Are they plotting a world takeover?
Or just waiting for dinner-sized pies?

What happened to my missing pen?
Did it roll off to meet a new fate?
Is there an office supply party?
Where all lost things gather and mate?

Questions That Linger

Why do we call it a driveway?
When all we do is park all day?
Should we change the name to sitway?
Because it's where we lounge and sway.

If money doesn't grow on trees,
Why aren't there rich forests around?
Maybe coins dangle from branches,
And we just haven't looked on the ground?

What dreams do jellybeans dream?
Of racing with chocolate and cream?
Or do they worry about the squish?
In a world where flavors can teem?

Do fish ever get thirsty, I wonder?
Do they long for a gulp of the air?
Or are they swimming in blissful thoughts,
In oceans where questions might flare?

A Season of Unanswered Riddles

Where does the sun put its hat?
At the end of the day, what's its style?
Is it a fedora, or maybe a cap?
Worn while it shines for a while?

Do we really need to count sheep?
Or does counting them spoil the night?
Maybe they'll just hop over fences,
And we'll be stuck with this fright?

If the sky is so far away,
How do stars manage to twinkle?
Do they wink with a touch of mischief?
Or is it all just one big sprinkle?

Can ducks get our weather updates?
With their quacks sharing news from afar?
Do they laugh when it rains on our picnic,
Taking off with our crumbs in a car?

The Stillness of Unsure Waters

A fish flipped, wearing a frown,
Wondering why it can't swim upside down.
The bubbles popped like awkward chats,
As if the pond held all the spats.

The turtles debated what lay ahead,
One claimed fish had a secret thread.
The ducks just quacked, quite out of tune,
While frogs pondered how to dance at noon.

The lily pads floated with puzzled glee,
Contemplating life like it's a quiz esprit.
But under the surface, it's all a show,
Unsure waters, what do they know?

In stillness, they drift, seeking the truth,
No map or compass for this pool of sleuth.
They splash and they giggle, repeat the jest,
Beats me what's next, let's just take a rest!

Embracing the Grey

At dawn, I wore socks of mismatched hue,
Wondering if style is a riddle or two.
The sun peeped out, with a look quite sly,
Dressed in gray, under the confused sky.

Is it fashion or folly? I can't really tell,
These shades add a twist to my morning carousel.
Why choose black or white when gray is so fun?
A color of questions, a mix of sun or gun.

In the street, folks glance, then they smile wide,
As I walk past in my plaid with pride.
Their laughter rings out like a melody,
Is it laughter at me, or just harmony?

So here's to the gray, ever the shade,
In a world full of choices, it never does fade.
Yes, I'll embrace all the colors that sway,
In the midst of confusion, I'll frolic and play!

The Weight of Silence

In a room full of chatter, I pause for a snack,
As everyone whispers, I feel a bit whack.
What's deeply unsaid weighs heavy like bread,
But giggles escape, that's how laughter is bred.

The clock ticks loudly, yet nobody shares,
With a sandwich in hand, I'm caught in their stares.
Can whispers feel weighty, like a thick old tome?
In the silence, I crunch; it sounds like a poem.

A voice breaks through with a pun that falls flat,
"Did you hear silence is heavier than that?"
We burst into chuckles; the room shakes with glee,
It's funny how silence can lighten the spree.

So here's to the quiet, that's never quite clear,
Let's fill it with laughter, that's how we veer.
With each jest we toss, we lighten the load,
In a world full of questions, let's lighten the road!

Beyond What the Heart Knows

Oh, the heart says one thing, but the mind's on a spree,
Chasing its tail like a dog lost at sea.
Does it lead to wisdom, or simply a mess?
My soul's throwing darts; oh, where do they bless?

Knocking on doors that don't seem to be there,
The mind whispers secrets, but really, who cares?
Hopscotch on feelings, a game of charades,
The questions we dance through, in comical spades.

With socks on my hands and a hat on my feet,
I juggle assumptions, a whimsical feat.
"Are you mad?" they all ask, while I juggle with grace,
It's fun being silly, in this questioning race.

Yet even with shenanigans, one truth doesn't sway,
Our hearts can be silly in a glorious way.
So let's ask the questions, embrace every quirk,
For beyond what we know lies a whole lot of work!

In the Silence of Unsaid Words

Why did the chicken cross that road?

To ponder if it could code!
Yet it forgot the punchline there,
And ended up caught in the glare.

What do ducks think, I don't know,
While quacking about their next show.
Could it be deep philosophical quips,
Or just a plan for some water trips?

When I asked my dog, he just yawned,
As if my musings left him pawned.
Now I'm here, with my pensive jive,
Turns out, unanswered thoughts keep alive.

So if you see a cow in a suit,
Wondering why it doesn't hoot,
Just know it's pondering the stars,
Or perhaps how to drive fancy cars!

Whispers of the Unknown

Why do socks disappear in the wash?

Is it a secret, a catchy posh?
Maybe they're off on a grand spree,
To find out what it's like to be free.

I asked a toaster about bread's fate,
It just popped out and shrugged in wait.
Are toasters involved in some sly scheme?
Or just buttering up for a dream?

When the clock ticks backward, what's the chance?
Maybe time is just a funky dance.
"Twenty-four hours? Nah, try eight!"
That's when my mind begins to flate.

The cat sits there, with a wise glare,
I swear, he knows the answers fair.
But he just stretches, gives a yawn,
And leaves me with questions till dawn.

The Weight of Half-Formed Thoughts

I ponder if a fish can sing,

Or if it's just a flapping fling.
Do they have dreams of flying high?
Or just swim along, wondering why?

A snail once told me he has speed,
Though he's no sprinter, take heed.
Is he racing life at his own pace,
Or just enjoying a slimy grace?

What do you get if you cross a bear?
A hairy question, a fuzzy scare!
Nonsense solutions stack on my shelf,
And I can't help but question myself.

The fridge hums tunes of lost delights,
It serenades us through the nights.
I suspect it knows the secret quest,
But it feigns indifference, just like the rest!

Shadows of Curiosity

Why does a shadow follow me tight?

Is it a friend or a buggering fright?
Does it have plans that I don't know?
Or simply waiting for light to show?

I once asked the moon about its day,
It chuckled softly, "I just stray."
Do the stars have gossip they share?
Or do they hide secrets beyond compare?

When I saw a squirrel with nuts galore,
I pondered just what it was for.
Is it a stash for winter's delight?
Or an office party gone out of sight?

Curiosity pulls me by the ear,
Teasing truths that aren't so clear.
Yet, here I sit, with my quirky frown,
And laugh at the riddles the world drowns down.

Navigating the Dark Waters

In the deep of the night, I lost my keys,
Chasing shadows that dance in the breeze.
Is that a ghost or just my cat?
I'll never know, so I'll just sit and chat.

The fridge hums a tune, so sweet,
While leftover pizza can't be beat.
But where'd the socks go? It's quite a game—
Perhaps the dryer is to blame.

I ponder the moon, as it hangs so bright,
Does it ever get tired shining all night?
Questions abound like stars in a list,
But answers are things that I can't twist.

Where's that odd smell? Is it lunch or a shoe?
I'll launch an expedition, maybe with a crew.
Though the waters are dark and the path is unclear,
At least I'll have laughs and a slice of beer!

The Void of Potential

In the fridge where leftovers reside,
I find mystery meals I try to hide.
Each Tupperware holds secrets galore,
What was that dish? I can't take it anymore!

The dust bunnies dance like they're on parade,
While I scheme on the couch, plans left unpaid.
Should I clean or just chill with a snack?
Decisions are hard; my mind starts to crack.

The remote's gone missing; it's under a book,
Who knew such a treasure could live where it's took?
Questions arise like socks in a wash,
Each one a puzzle, a strange and funny posh.

Why does my cat think the closet's a den?
Is it a cave, or just my old pen?
Potential for chaos in every small space,
Still I'll smile wide, lost in this grace!

The Mystery Around Us

Why do we trip on flat, solid ground?
Is gravity plotting? Have we been bound?
I swear that last step wasn't there at all,
But it chuckled softly as I took the fall.

Blocking my thoughts with a snack on the side,
I ponder the meaning of socks that collide.
Why are they magic, disappearing so quick?
It's a sock-thieving monster, that's the trick!

The clocks in my house don't seem to agree,
Ticking away, but never with glee.
Do they sense time's a slippery blur?
Or are they just plotting? Oh, who would concur?

A toaster that burns bread as a regular feat,
The coffee's a mystery that just can't be beat.
In this tangled web of everyday lore,
Laughter's the treasure, I keep coming back for!

Embracing the Abyss

As I sit on the couch with my feet on the floor,
I dive through my thoughts, oh, I must explore!
Are my plants alive or just having a dream?
With questions like these, coffee's my theme.

The cat's plotting schemes from her throne on the shelf,
While I question deeply the meaning of self.
Am I just a spectator in my own funny show?
Or is every odd moment a script I must know?

The vacuum hums softly, it whispers and shouts,
Is it cleaning the house or just casting doubts?
I swear it's conspiring, but then it must be,
Just another contraption dreading its spree.

So let's raise a glass to unanswered things,
And toast to the joy that each question brings.
For in the abyss where the odd shadows play,
Laughter is gold; let it brighten the day!

Step into the Unknown

I took a step, tripped on my shoe,
What answers await? I've no clue.
A fortune cookie said to explore,
But all I found was an open door.

I ask the cat why it stares at me,
Is it a sage or just hungry?
A talking goldfish swims in a bowl,
Giving advice? Just a fish with a goal.

So many mysteries, I can't even begin,
Like why my toast lands butter-side in.
With questions baked in, I laugh and I spin,
Perhaps the real treasure lies deep within.

A puzzling map that leads to nowhere,
Each twist and turn, a humorous scare.
In the great unknown, I jest and jest,
The laughter I find feels like a quest.

Faces of Untold Stories

A man at the bus stop wears mismatched shoes,
His smile suggests he knows hidden hues.
I wonder his tale—does he dance in the rain?
Or is he a pirate, just searching for fame?

A lady with a hat that's shaped like a cake,
Could she be a baker? For goodness' sake!
As if asking her question might make it come true,
I wave from afar—what a strange view!

And there's a fellow with glasses too big,
Each time he sneezes, it's quite the jig!
I ponder if laughter's the glue that we need,
Or just a big joke that's destined to lead.

With faces like these, oh what can I say?
The quirkiest stories are out every day.
In this world full of laughs and a shrug, I'll reprise,
Each untold story, a playful surprise.

Hues of Mysterious Thought

I found a thought in a sock pile today,
It wore a bright hat, said, 'Come out and play!'
It danced in circles, tripped on a beam,
Turning mundane into a whimsical dream.

A question rose up painted azure blue,
Said, 'Who decided that Mondays are true?'
I scribbled a note on a napkin, you see,
Perhaps I'll pop questions like bubbles in tea.

These hues of thought swirl like candy in air,
While I ponder why squirrels with acorns just stare.
Each answer eludes like a feather on breeze,
My brain is a canvas; I paint it with ease.

In shades of confusion, I chuckle and grin,
Each whimsical wonder just sparks from within.
For splashes of laughter color my quest,
In this wacky palette, I feel so blessed.

Questions Like Falling Leaves

Questions cascade like leaves in the fall,
Swirling and twirling, they dance at my call.
I wonder if trees chat with each wobbly breeze,
Or if squirrels spin plots to steal all their cheese.

As I rake the yard, I find one that reads,
'Why do we chase after unfulfilled needs?'
A leaf whispers back, with a flutter and twist,
'Maybe it's better to live in the mist.'

Each rustling question carries a jest,
While pondering life, I chuckle and rest.
The humor of pondering an answer so far,
Is like asking a snail why it's not a car.

So here I stand, questions scattered like seeds,
In laughter and joy, I gather my leads.
With autumn's confusion, oh what a reprieve,
For questions like leaves, I gladly receive.

Nightfall of Questions

Why does my cat stare at the wall?
Is she plotting my fall or a grand cat ball?
The fridge hums secrets, deep in its dark,
But all I want is a snack, not a quirk or a lark.

Do socks have a magical run?
Where do they hide? Is it just for fun?
I search for answers, lost in a trance,
While they dance 'round the dryer, in their own little dance.

The sky keeps trying to change its hue,
Yet here I am, stuck in this shoe.
Is it fate or a cosmic joke?
I laugh with the stars; they must love to poke.

In this circus of thoughts, I take it all light,
'Cause without the strange questions, what's day without night?
Maybe it's better, to grin and to chuckle,
For laughter, my friend, is the best sort of puzzle.

The Beauty of an Open Mind

Why is the sky blue and why are we here?
Every question answered brings more fear.
Like puzzles that grow, they twist and they bend,
I giggle at how they never quite end.

My toaster's got quirks, it pops with a song,
Is it trying to join the breakfast throng?
Or is it lost in a caffeine-less day,
Trying to butter me up in a toast-dreamy way?

I gaze at the plants that talk to the breeze,
Do they whisper sweet nothings to the gossiping trees?
Perhaps they debate if the sun came too late,
As I sip my coffee and wait for fate.

A world full of questions is fun to explore,
Pondering life over pancakes galore.
So let's lift our forks and join in the jest,
Who needs all the answers? We're on quite the quest!

Heartbeats of Doubt

Do fish have a plan when they swim in a row?
Or do they just follow the bubbles that blow?
I ponder their motives while I munch on my snack,
Should I follow fish vibes or just chill and relax?

Why do we look for logic in socks that go missing?
Are they out on adventures, or just nonchalantly kissing?
Perhaps they're stuck in a sock-a-grab game,
While I keep on searching, well that's just my fame!

Bubbles in soda are sneaky, I swear,
They giggle when popped; do they really care?
I watch them bounce up, all joyful and free,
Is the answer to life found in fizz? Just maybe!

Doubt fills my mind as I laugh at the quirks,
'Cause who needs a handbook for life's little perks?
Let's dance with confusion; it's all part of the art,
And with every weird question, it makes life a part.

Chasing Shadows of Clarity

Why does my dog bark at each passing car?
Is he trying to warn me, or just a pet star?
Sometimes he howls at the moon in delight,
Perhaps he's chasing shadows in the dead of night.

Do clouds ever wonder where all the rain goes?
Or do they just float and exchange secret prose?
I watch as they drift, a vague mystery,
Do they giggle at us, pondering history?

A fork in the road asks me which way to trot,
I laugh and I ponder, 'Guess I'll just keep what I've got!'
For each twist and turn holds a giggle or two,
Life's a great riddle, in which dreams come true.

So here's to the questions, let's raise up a toast,
For clarity lives in the shadows we boast.
Chasing answers is fun; what's a joke without jest?
In the dance of the unknown, we're truly the best!

Ribbons of Mystery

Why did the chicken cross the road?
To find out what it owed!
But every step it took just led,
To questions swirling in its head.

The socks I lost, where do they go?
A portal to the socky show?
I check the dryer, poke and pry,
But all I find is lint and sighs.

Do cats really rule the night,
In secret meetings out of sight?
They plot their world domination,
Yet nap all day in contemplation.

If bubbles pop, do they get old?
Or are they stories yet untold?
I blow a bubble, watch it soar,
And laugh at life's absurd decor.

The Depths of Anticipation

I left my keys somewhere, oh dear!
They didn't say goodbye, I fear.
Is that a ghost or just a chair?
My mind plays tricks everywhere!

I planned a meal with fishy flair,
But hoped for beef, so not quite fair.
Now here I am with a plate of tuna,
Trying to act like a real food boomer!

What's hiding in that odd-shaped box?
Could it be cheese or maybe socks?
A mystery wrapped in foil so tight,
I poke and prod, start a small fight.

Why do shoes always lose their mates?
I swear they're having secret dates!
While I'm stuck here with one alone,
They're two-stepping to a party unknown.

Amidst the Unanswered Labyrinth

I took a walk down memory lane,
But got lost in a silly game.
The path is winding, full of woe,
Where is that thing I ought to know?

Why does my phone autocorrect?
To words that cause me pure neglect?
I text my friends a laugh or two,
And they reply, 'What did you do?'

I tried to bake a cake today,
But mixed the salt with flour, yay!
Now serving up a salty brew,
My friends all cheer, 'Oh, what's new?'

If I could ask the stars above,
Why it's so hard to find true love?
They wink and twirl, just a tease,
As I ponder, can't catch that breeze.

The Journey Without a Map

I set out with a plan, oh me!
But directions, no, they weren't for me.
I took a turn and found a cat,
Who looked at me like, 'What's up with that?'

The compass spun like a dancer's twirl,
Leading me deeper into a whirl.
Is that a sign or just a rock?
I check my watch and hear a clock.

I came upon a sign so bright,
That said, 'You're lost! What a delight!'
It leaned and chuckled, quite the joke,
As I just stood there, slightly choked.

With every twist my mind goes wild,
Like a little lost and wandering child.
But in this maze, I find pure glee,
For who needs maps when you've got me?

The Labyrinth of Inquiries

In a maze of thoughts, I wander around,
Searching for answers that can't be found.
Why is the sky blue? Is toast a lie?
Spinning in circles, I just ask why.

Questions like popcorn, they pop in my head,
Did I leave the oven on? Am I well-fed?
I thought I'd be wise, but here I just stand,
In a world full of wonders, I just misplanned.

Are cats really plotting to take over the scene?
Or are they just napping, living the dream?
I ponder the meaning of socks that go missing,
Leaving me puzzled, but maybe just wishing.

With each silly query, I giggle a bit,
As I trip on my thoughts, a comedic skit.
In the labyrinth of musings where answers grow shy,
I dance with confusion, oh my oh my!

When Answers Go Awry

Last night I asked, what's the meaning of life?
My cat just stared like a wise little wife.
I tried to decode her enigmatic gaze,
But all I got back was a bewildered daze.

I once asked a toaster why it spits bread,
It popped up a slice and just laughed instead.
Are kitchen appliances in on the joke?
If so, I need answers...or maybe a poke.

Why do socks vanish? Are they in a war?
Did they plot with the spoons to escape through the door?

Everywhere searching for that sneaky thief,
Just a mundane life mixed with absurd beliefs.

In the comedy show of my mind's little play,
Questions bobble like popcorn that won't go away.
With each tick of the clock, I giggle and sigh,
What's the answer, my friend? Oh goodness, O my!

Glimpses Behind the Curtain

Behind the curtain, what do I see?
A family of answers, not one wants to be.
They peek out and giggle, then vanish from sight,
The elusive little critters, what a funny fight!

I asked the universe, "Where's the remote?"
It winked at me slyly, and then floated a boat.
Questions like kites, they fly up and away,
And I'm here on the ground, just stuck with my say.

Every riddle I face feels like a big joke,
Like asking a chicken if she'll fly or choke.
The mysteries dance in a whimsical tune,
While I scribble my queries beneath the bright moon.

So here's to the riddles, the jokes on the side,
With laughter and wonder, I take them in stride.
When answers elude me, I'll still raise a cheer,
For the fun of the chase is what brings me near!

Navigating the Unfathomable

A GPS for questions? I wish it was true,
But it only leads me to 'Where's the loo?'
Every twist and turn feels like a grand prank,
The map of my thoughts—oh, what a blank!

I thought I had reason; I had it all planned,
Then my mind rebelled and just waved its hand.
"Find your own pathway through this silly mess!"
And I'm stuck on a riddle, which I must confess.

Why do we ponder? Is it part of the game?
Each silly inquiry feels just the same.
With laughter as fuel, I roam through this haze,
Chasing after questions through a humorous maze.

So here I am, with a shrug and a grin,
As I dance with my thoughts, I feel the spin.
Though answers stay hidden, I don't mind the hunt,
Life's a big riddle, and I'm just the font!

The Weight of Unresolved Dreams

In the fridge, a thought has brewed,
Last week's leftovers, feeling rude.
I ponder why socks always disappear,
They must be plotting, I fear!

Questions swirl like leaves in fall,
Why do we trip, then always stall?
Maybe the universe likes to tease,
Or it's just my clumsy knees.

I wonder how long a cat will stare,
At nothing but the empty air.
Are they seeing ghosts from the past?
Or just dreaming of a mouse feast vast?

In my head, a circus plays,
With elephants dancing in odd ballet.
I laugh at the whims of half-thought dreams,
Reality, it seems, is not what it seems.

Unraveled Threads of Inquiry

A sock mismatch leads to great debate,
Was it the dryer or a twist of fate?
I query why my coffee's cold,
As I rehearse the day's bold told.

The cat's insistence on attacking my feet,
Is it love or a sneaky little feat?
I seek answers in the crumbs of the past,
While my patience is fading fast.

Why do we giggle at our own puns?
As if laughter could calm our wild runs.
Is it wisdom or just a mirage?
In this game of thoughts, I'm a collage!

In the cupboard lies a mystery divine,
Why is there one spoon missing every time?
I may not solve all that's in my brain,
But I'll buy new spoons again and again.

Labyrinth of the Mind

Inside my head, a maze so wide,
With thoughts that twirl and often hide.
I chase them down with a frantic grin,
But they just laugh and spin, spin, spin!

Why does my toaster burn only one side?
Is it a feature or a secret guide?
I ponder deeply while munching my toast,
Whose invention deserves the most boast?

In the shadows lurks a thought so bright,
It dances around just out of sight.
Is there a map to this mental space?
Or do I keep running in this great race?

I find a joke tucked deep in my mind,
But the punchline's lost, I've tried to bind.
So I chuckle instead at my grim fate,
And start anew, it's never too late.

The Art of Not Knowing

With questions floating like helium balloons,
I often ponder my own cartoons.
Why can't I remember where I parked?
Is it my brain or the thief who sparked?

The search for answers is a wild game,
Like hunting for ninjas without a name.
I stand at the crossroads, lost in wonder,
As ducks in a row float by down under.

Why do I laugh at my garden weeds?
They sprout with glee in the sun, it leads.
Am I the gardener or just the fool?
In this comedy, I've made my rule.

I ponder if my plants have super thoughts,
As I offer them water in hopeful spots.
For in this world of unclear sight,
I'll smile at the chaos and dance with delight.

www.ingramcontent.com/pod-product-compliance
Lightning Source LLC
Chambersburg PA
CBHW051631160426
43209CB00004B/608